To the Left of the Sun

poems

To the Left of the Sun

poems

Linda Flaherty Haltmaier

HOMEBOUND PUBLICATIONS
Ensuring the Mainstream isn't the Only Stream

Homebound Publications
Ensuring the mainstream isn't the only stream
WWW.HOMEBOUNDPUBLICATIONS.COM

Published in 2018 ✦ Homebound Publications
Front Cover Image © James Scott Smith
Cover and Interior Designed by Leslie M. Browning
ISBN ✦ 978-1-947003-98-9
First Edition Trade Paperback

10 9 8 7 6 5 4 3 2 1

Homebound Publications is committed to ecological stewardship. We greatly value the
natural environment and invest in environmental conservation. Our books are printed
on paper with chain of custody certification from the Forest Stewardship Council,
Sustainable Forestry Initiative, and the Program for the
Endorsement of Forest Certification.

For Mom,
who lined our entire
house with bookshelves.
And for Dad,
who filled them.

Table of Contents

III. Circling the Open Field

IV. Whispers

V. Visiting Sparrows

Rumblings

Dead Birds

Bring me your dead birds,
drop them on the stoop
and together we'll sit
and marvel at their beauty
between sips of iced tea.

Others refuse to see the gifts
you lay at their feet, so rest here,
where it's safe—
We'll revel in the tenacity it took
to pluck this aerialist from the sky,
the heart required for such a hunt.

Dreams are hard catching
even for those with bent stick circles of
string and feather hanging on the door.
Their wrangling requires the
wild-eyed determination of a feline,
the cunning of a jackal—

Dreams are skittish and
spook easily into the bush,
where they like to hide out
biding their time until
the dreamer grows weary
or bored
or leaps in, finally,
claws bared.

Upon Reading Virginia Woolf's Suicide Note

It begins with *Dearest*
and ends with silence;
in between,
the choosing of the rocks—

Did she roll them in her hands
assessing their heft, their smoothness
like she was searching for the perfect skimming stone?
Or did she simply stuff her pockets
until the weight felt right,
just enough to pull her under,
even if her resolve faltered?

What was she thinking as
she looked out at the waters
about to become her home?
Waters that would swallow her brilliance
in one gulp like Jonah's whale,
a Roman candle doused
in a barrel of rainwater,

the river consuming a mind
that noticed everything, felt all,
turned experience into scratches on a page,
altering how women see themselves,
see the world.

Perhaps life had telescoped
into a pin-prick of darkness,
unrelenting,
words stripped of their protective buoyancy,
now heavy as the rocks
enlisted in their grim errand.

The Vermillion Border

sounds like a territory
the Gauls lost to the Romans,
a place of strife and barbed wire,
but instead, it's the curve
where cheek meets lip,
fair meets florid,
a demarcation,
a defining edge,
without which words would not form,
kisses would not be blown,
love might not be made.
Your lips hover over me,
blotting the sky
like a an errant zeppelin
in a Man Ray painting,
border set to be breached,
no permission needed.

Dangerous Women

There's a threat on the streets of Ankara
that erupts like an IED,
rippling in concentric circles,
swirling up towards the minarets,
a force that must be contained—

it rises up from the sidewalks,
women stream out for lunch,
headscarves and skirts flutter
into great, kaleidoscopic swallowtails,
drafting on secrets and fizz.
The wind carries their laughter

tinged with subversion,
schoolgirls in crisp uniforms
chase each other,
collapse in a pile of screeches,
their titters, like fingers on a keyboard
tapping out a contract,
I see you, you see me, we are bound together.

But the politics of women's joy
must be regulated—
women laughing in public
is a combustible force
an immodest display

that must be stamped out by men in Armani suits,
their facial hair a machismo prop,
their religion a Superman cape
donned to justify the silence they demand—
their greatest fear
that the laughter of women
is meant for them.

Vanishing Point

The line where ocean meets sky
wobbles like the mark of a freshman artist,
all straight lines destined to meet there,
that point sitting in infinity.

All rooftops and lamp posts and picture frames
will join up at the convergence,
their angles radiating outward,
straddling this world and the invisible

overlay of God's schematics.
We grease-pen in our theories,
trying to unravel beauty that befuddles,
patterns that smirk at randomness—

I held Fibonacci perfection in my hands
at the farmer's market the other day,
a type of cabbage I'd never seen,
its spokes alien and spiraling.

I cradled it,
the looping protrusions whispering
a mathematics I didn't understand.
I whispered back,
wishing I could speak in numbers.

The Solace of Dirt

What would I have told my father then,
a boy of thirteen, dog tired,
hands wrecked from digging graves–
as he watched a soda jerk spoon peanuts
onto his chocolate sundae?

Maybe I'd tell him that there was no solace coming,
no matter how many graves he dug,
no solace after this death, his mother's death,
not when a mother loved her son
with a Titanic-sized devotion,
huge, unwieldy, doomed.

Maybe I'd tell him that this after-school job,
an odd choice for grief so fresh,
for one so recently burdened, wasn't going to help,
that there wasn't a hole big enough to contain the loss,

that the dark earth ground into his pants,
the same dirt that held her in ghastly repose,
couldn't be cleaned out, not ever—

that the taint of dirt and death and grief
would be a forever stain across generations,
and that ice cream would never taste right again,
no matter how many peanuts were piled on it.

This Day

Some days are chop wood,
carry water days,
no flourish,
no grand embellishment,
just the business of the day
taken moment by moment,
task by task.
A broom scratches across the floor,
clothes dance a soapy two step,
plates clank into place,

Sparrows do their version
outside the kitchen window,
they flit and squeak,
beaks full, then not—

A house finch fusses over a whisker of dried grass,
hopping a jig of indecision
until he clamps down and zips off,
perhaps to build a mini Versailles for his love,
a monument of twig and dander
set in the crook of a dinosaur-skinned oak.

Or maybe there's a drafty spot that needs fixing—
I wonder about the hatchlings
this blade will keep warm and dry,
and if they'll make the pilgrimage
back to my scruffy yard
when the air mellows and mud is king again—

to pad their first lopsided nests
with relics of winter's end.
The samsara wheel clicks another click
as hands cup suds,
a mind caught mid-flight,
thankful for a day in this sturdy little house.

Cracks

I imagine my scars spackled in gold,
like a ceramic pot repaired with reverence,
an object worthy of a Kintsugi restoration,
the damage turned radiant,
criss-crossing seams
circling
flashing at the place where knife edge met skin.
A story of dits and dashes,
pauses in a fleshy covering
that irridesce at the slightest movement.
Each ding
honors the resilience of this sturdy vessel.
Each crack
leaves a trace of the healing voodoo
that knit flesh and bone back into human.
Ancient Egyptians called gold
the skin of the gods—
I squint at the mirror as light
flickers off me,
and for a moment,
imagine this body as precious
as an artifact in Tutankhamen's tomb.

The Reliquary of Lost Friendship

The memories
are propped up on tiny stands
like Madagascar hissing beetles
and Kachina dolls,
tilting relics,
curiosities of the heart under glass.

One sharp puff and
I'm back on the playground,
rolling a rubber ball
to the kicker at home plate—
one eye on first base,
where my best friend stands ready,

The title of best friend,
conferred onto the chosen
like Supreme Court Justice or Senator,
with less fanfare but no less gravity.
It guaranteed play dates and sleep overs,
secrets kept,
inside jokes and laughing fits,
a bond unquestioned.

Until one morning,
I awoke to find that the plates beneath me
had shifted,
landed me in an unfamiliar longitude
where this friendship,

once formidable as a triceratops,
was no longer a living thing—
the breath that animated
the love between us had gone stale,
the gods had taken back their lightning.

It wasn't the last time it happened,
but the first was the most baffling
to an inexperienced heart,
not savvy about the tender magic
that weaves a dandelion yoke of friendship,
and then unravels it without warning.

Others took their place on the shelf,
friends from overnight camp,
freshman year of college,
that first job in New York City—
each one labeled, dated, prized,
secrets intact.

Up and Out

The birds sense it first,
the energy rising from the
damp earth,
the scratching of roots—
maples, field grass,
desiccated tiger lilies
ready for re-animation.
Pulpy fingerlings
shake off the chill,
annoying a beetle out
of his stupor—
to wobble his way
up through the soil
to the radiating warmth,
carapace glinting
like the hood of a '67 Mustang
in need of a good scrub—
his antennae alert for
the rumblings of life
erupting all around,
daring the birds
to stay preoccupied
with their flirting
and fluttering
in the glow
of spring's new day.

Terra Incognita

She studies my face for a sign,
a greeting to alert her
to where she is in space,
how she fits into the orbit of today,

her clothes too big
the world too fast
reality too elusive.
My hand lights on a

morning glory of purple that
flowered on her arm
since last visit,
a Rorschach of dried blood

beneath skin no thicker than a dragonfly wing.
If I look long enough
I may see straight through
to chambered bone

or nerves tinged scarlet,
wrapped around highways of blue—
She is the Lucite model
from my fourth grade Christmas list,

The Visible Woman marked with four stars,
the highest magnitude of want,

a see-through shell of parts
color-coded for easy identification.

She never landed under the tree,
Malibu Barbie showed up instead,
the cartography of the body
still inscrutable as runes.

Among Us

Did you know you that were a God?
With your handlebar mustache,
plaid Sansabelt slacks and sucked-in paunch—
To my third grade eyes, that hadn't seen much
beyond Scooby-Doo and the Natick Mall,
you were all that and a bag of chips, 70's style.

You rolled into the kitchen each night
with hollowed-out eyes
we weren't supposed to notice,
ones that sputtered like a dying flashlight
as kids and dogs pounced their greeting,
a briefcase tilting you ever starboard.

Mom lifted her chin at the stove
for her peck on the cheek,
then I'd pull you back out the door,
Frankenstein wingtips crunching
a path to the side yard
where tomatoes and zucchini
blushed radioactive in the creeping twilight.

I'd count the bounty,
report back on ripeness and redness,
squeal about baby tomatoes,
tiny pale orbs still nestled in their starry caps—

You'd stand, thumb over nozzle,
drenching Jurassic leaves
like a carny sharp-shooter,
the apricot-dusted blooms and
your button-down safe from soaking
in some kind of magic–

I'd hold up a monster zucchini
like a prizewinning trout
and you'd look over,
a wow on your lips,
battery and filament connecting,
beam holding steady.

Beyond the Trees

Unspeakable

Thoughts pop into my head
that would make Mussolini blanch,
mass judgments,
comments worthy of Ivory soap intervention,
dictums on the basic intelligence of this
flawed and flabby life form.
I could be ruler of this planet
my inner ten-year-old squeals
with Trumpian fervor,
the surge of arrogance palpable.

And then, it's as if the Dalai Llama himself nudges my head—
A father and his autistic son are crossing the street,
laughing, tussling—
love arcing between them like a Tesla coil,
and for a moment these flawed and flabby creatures
seem noble and generous,
capable of blinding grace,
unspeakable kindness.

I blink away a tear and pull into traffic,
a driver whizzes past, too close,
moment curdled,
mic hijacked by a Commandant
with a filthy mouth.

Deflated

Summer's sweaty grip loosens,
granting last bike rides,
final trips to the beach,
and cherry popsicles laced with dread—
it's the dead-man-walking time of summer,
the ticking down of days
louder than the peepers' surging July din.
The pendulum swoosh sends
a first morning chill
through the bedroom window,
covers pulled up tight,
harbinger of soccer games,
cider donuts, and stiff collars
on picture day.

Tell Me

If I were to heave up my innards for you,
liver, kidney, spleen,
right here in this kitchen,
splat plunk on this oak table,
would it be enough?
Pull my intestines out like
a magician's scarf,
all twenty-two feet of them,
drape them over the kitchen cabinets
like twinkle lights,
then splosh my heart into
the glass bowl we got for our wedding,
the one where pears
ripen and rot each week
waiting to be chosen—
Could we call it even then?

A Word, please

Is your God
my God?
Does he or she call the deer
to nibble on the
piney spokes of the spruce?
Send jellyfish to bloom into
a quivering armada?
Turn poppy fields
into sheets of molten red
undulating by the roadside in Provence?
Either way, I'd like to have a word.
I want to know how it all ends—
the trees,
the oceans,
the hawks circling,
the lady bug on my window.

Untethered

Loud voices,
pounding footsteps—
I can't hear Laverne or Shirley,
the volume knob miles from the couch.
Then a crash from above,

terror screams down the stairs
into the TV room,
like Medusa herself—
turning flesh to stone,
a laugh-track swelling
in unregistered hilarity.

My brother takes the stairs two at a time,
my Keds tripping close behind.
He stops short at my bedroom.
Dad is straddling my sister,
a wild mustang beneath him
pinned to a flowered bedspread.

Her transgressions have pulled
the pin on his rage, again.
His arms wheel at her,
she flails, frenzied.
Silent witnesses hold, frozen,
dutiful palace guards outside a door,
now a gateway to hell.

My tiny tea-cup voice croaks—
Daddy, stop it.
Mom pushes through,
I feel my lungs want to breathe again,
help is here, hang on.

She barrels in to the far window,
past the bed and without a glance,
snaps the shade closed in one quick jerk,
a guillotine falling into its slot—
she glides over and yanks the other down.

The shades make a grating sound,
like rusty kitchen scissors ripping
through bone and gristle
and the very laws of nature.

I feel my sneakers lift,
watch them float up towards my head
as I somersault backwards,
tumble past the popcorn ceiling
and puffy pink insulation
into the night sky—

A doll-sized Mom walks down
the stairs straightening her shirt.
No one notices
as I spin off into the twinkle-lit void,
no longer a resident
of 7 Middlesex Street,
or planet earth.

Lost and Found

I lost myself, she says,
as if she were a stuffed animal
left at a bus station.
Women on talk shows are always
lamenting the loss of themselves.
Maybe we need a GPS for that,
one with a snooty British accent—
In 2.4 miles take a right onto Main Street.
In 200 feet, arrive at your destination.
There on a street lined with maples,
you'll find yourself sitting on a park bench
throwing bits of crust to brown squirrels.
The kids, the husband, the life in service to others,
drowned out by the deafening sound
of grass stretching toward sky.

On Demand

Come on, honey, give me a smile,
says the man outside the bodega,
my face slack as a marionette
dangling on a nail,

the intricate choreography of a dozen muscles,
defiantly blasé,
a grin in repose.
The mechanics, a porridge of Latin names,
Zygomaticus major in charge—

But I don't owe this stranger or this world
my smile,
my pretty,
my perfected body.

Tugging on cables that bare my teeth
to placate and fit in,
lemurs, gorillas, chimpanzees,
furry brethren,
all consider smiling an act of aggression,
a menacing display of dental prowess.

So today I'll navigate with the ancestors,
slip through the city streets
flashing a hint of incisor on my terms—
ready for an unexpected delight
to trip this complex system
of rigs and pulleys,
baring all.

The Dark Triad

Cross-legged in a cardboard box,
the brook churning a froth of rust and slime,
she peers out of the container,
spoils of an epic tug-of-war with her sister,
now her ship, The Maytag,
mummified in sheets of cling wrap,
trussed with Scotch tape, twine,
and unbounded optimism.

This time, the waters won't soak her shorts or
wreck her paisley suitcase full of
penny candy and stuffed animals.

This time, the seeping chill won't stop her,
these red sneakers will speed
down the current,
racing chubby tadpoles as bullfrogs bellow
their goodbyes.

This time, she's off to a distant land beyond the trees,
beyond the edge of the known world,
to a place of quiet,
where the earth is padded with pine needles
and smells of sap and new flowers.

This time, she'll stay gone as long as she can,
build a bed of Catalpa leaves
and lay her head on a dandelion pillow,
the stars her only night light.

This time, maybe they'll notice she's gone before dark.
Her sister told her to watch out,
that people disappear in the Bermuda Triangle,
but she's not worried—
there's a wilted clump in her pocket,
a four leaf clover from the backyard.

Meta-morphosis

Gregor Samsa may have been on to something,
morphing into a giant beetle,
his wing casings the size of car doors,
sturdy, armored—
not like our sweaty flesh costumes
too flimsy for a world teeming
with careless screen-watchers,
their palms turned ever-inwards,
posing to selfie every moment—
the undocumented life not worth living.
I think about the apple lodged in Gregor's side,
there to rot and humiliate.
I want to yank it out for him,
his spiny, forked legs
clacking on the oak floors, useless.

Laying Hands on the Emptiness

She grieves for the invisible wrongs,
the ghosts of lack,
the specters of what should have been,
the manna that never made it to her table.
Their absence stings just below the skin,
where bruises of the soul leave their mark—
no corpuscles smashed into flowering,
no blood trail to follow
no overt sign of damage,
just the belly of innocence constricting,
a bitter sap weeping into the empty spaces,
threatening to harden,
the residue sticky and unforgiving.

Wormhole

Death is trying to find a way in—
vulture hawks circle
like Hare Krishnas at the airport,
bells tinkling
as John Donne's promised crescendo looms.

Death doesn't want me,
not yet anyway,
but he smells the sweet decay,
the blood in the water,
the reek of inevitability emitted by
the crumpled lady in the wheelchair—
once a mighty warrior at the stove,
a mom with answers, Band-Aids,
and whoopie pies to make everything okay.

She's in the crosshairs now—
and death, a patient sniper,
is loaded with coffee and sandwiches
for a long stake out,
a bag of grim tools by his side.
A small sore has given him entree,
breached the hull—
his minions will taste their
meal soon enough.

Circling the
Open Field

Dear Poetry Editor

I submit for your approval
words on a page as
juicy and brimming as follicles in an ovary,
ideas as unrepentant as stones,
images that strobe against cranial walls
like a motel TV on the fritz.
Here they are laid out for you
to stamp yea or nay,
to harvest or to salt—
these words with glossy berries
to lure you in
and prickers to make you bleed.
I crave the recoil,
the gasp,
the flush of recognition
that spreads faster than a single malt—
careful, there might be a metaphor
in stanza three cunning as a trap door spider,
or a sublime simile up ahead that will
have you questioning your God—
I humbly await your submission.

Aftertaste

He showed her the beauty of a begonia,
how to plant zucchini seeds in a mound,
not too many or they'll strangle each other,
fed her books like caramels—
unleashed the genius of Jules Verne and
H.G. Wells into her imagination.

Afternoons spent curled up together
as Mothra toppled Tokyo or
giant ants threatened mankind.
He recited poems until they stuck—
All in a hot and copper sky, the bloody sun at noon,

Taught her the clean lines of Art Deco,
the inventions of Da Vinci,
how JFK killed the hat industry.

His mind, a funhouse of riches and color—
with a side-show tent of terrors out back.
Moods capricious and violent—
how they curdled the cotton candy,
ground ash into the caramel apples.

Lithium makes men impotent
he scoffed once when she was old
enough to understand,
a diabolical calculus
that unmanned his legacy as a father,
left a trail of broken daughters in his wake,

wary of men, confused about love,
burdened with a darkness not their own.

The memories are like the Hershey bar
he kept stashed in the fridge
behind an open can of sauerkraut,
faintly sweet
and laced with strong vinegar.

The Nest

I gather twigs and sticks,
broken bits of blue glass,
shards that kaleidoscope
and confuse the red-tailed hawk
circling the open field
where I left my heart.
A rogue organ—
independent and vulnerable,
it needs tending and a place to rest.
I tuck fluff and dander in the
empty spaces between the dried grass,
allowing just enough light
to get through.

A Meandering Mind

What happens to a mind tied to a post,
never let off its leash
to roam the byways and coasts and tributaries
of its own contours?

Moments scooped out of the day,
in line at the grocery store,
at a red light,
moments when a mind can slip off its tether
and wander,
muse about the boy in algebra,
puzzle over why that woman
picked that hat out of all the hats in hatdom.

Stooped heads and busy fingers
have replaced these walkabouts,
a mind disconnected from its own thoughts,
off-loading functions to binary code,
cascading vines of 1's and 0's
strangle tender shoots of creation.

Mislaid moments that jolt a mind awake
like Frankenstein's cables—
A top-heavy tulip bobbing by the roadside,
Autumn light spilling off a sugar maple,
all missed,

eyes lodged in the palm of a hand
like loaded dice—
the spark of creation snuffed out
by a thoughtless like
and a smiling emoji.

Choosing my father's casket

A plain pine box,
nothing fancy,
he said,
funeral directors are
just vultures in bad ties,

But when the time came,
he wasn't there to take on the shiny suit
that spoke in a breathy whisper,
like Marilyn Monroe singing
Happy Birthday, Mr. President,

and led us to a dim room.
Caskets hung from the wall,
back-lit for effect,
stacked like bunk beds in a
teen horror flick.

I brayed at the threshold,
instincts rearing—
my sisters filed past,
offerings glowed
in the amber fluorescence,

They oohed and ahhed,
distracted from
the sudden crack of grief
that is unexpected death,
that tasered us

into a new world order
of burial plots and grave markers,
price tags spun,
opinions ricocheted,
until they formed a semi-circle

around a blue-gray model
and looked over at me,
a coven of sad witches
seeking consecration.

100 Inches and Counting

An inside cat,
that's what I've become.
Yawning away the morning
as another storm blusters through,
I curl up at the window
to watch the politics
of goldfinches and blue jays
as they vie for prime spots
at the feeder,
the antagonist,
a furry acrobat
with plans to up-end the party and
shower the seeds to the frozen ground.
Birds flutter off to smaller trees
still mummified in snow,
trunks encased in icy wraps.
Only today, the buds on the
branch tips have changed—
dragon lady fingernails
point skyward in the swirl,
promising an end to this
muffled, inside existence.
Soon, winter will trickle
into storm drains
along with salty tales told
of the winter when snow banks
were higher than roof tops.

James Bond at the Memory Ward

Are you familiar with the James Bond series?
she asks, eyes gleaming with a secret.
Sean Connery is right over there.
She points to a stooped man with a grey beard
shuffling into the dining room.
Really? I say.
Yep, he's filming his new movie here.
I squint hard until the memory care facility,
James Bond, and everything in it
fractals into a Monet blur.
By God, that does look like 007.

Cloud Theory

So this is what love is,
like clouds assembling
and disassembling
into an elephant,
a three-legged turtle,
a lopsided dragon's head,
then gone,
leaving a swath of disordered blue—

Not like the clouds I drew
with my sacred box of 64—
scalloped, identical puffs,
always to the left of the sun,
lemon yellow spokes blazing for
the tulips below,
stems caught mid-curtsey,
grateful for the warmth.

Some learn early on that love
is a not a new puppy
or never having to say you're sorry.
It's more like a merry-go-round
with a stuck lever,
the hung-over attendant smoking a butt,
oblivious to the kids hanging on for dear life,
their faces smashed into fiberglass manes
that reek of sweat and popcorn,
willing it to stop.

Election Results

The trees don't know who won or lost—
they stand,
rooted and flaming,
dropping leaves
that gold plate the earth
like the walls of a Buddhist temple.

Kim Crawford Isn't Welcome Here Anymore...

And tell her pals Mark West
and Jed Steele that the party is over,
time to take the shindig elsewhere.
How fun it was to sip and swirl,
inhale sophistication with a deep sniff,
spouting words like earthy, ripe, buttery
in all earnestness,
a light pear undertone,
a hint of clay,
sounding oh so clever on evenings
when words flowed like the wine.
That innocent glass before dinner,
the glug of the pour,
prelude to a liquid symphony
about to spread Brahms throughout
my body,
thirsty nerve endings primed to sigh,
a ritualistic Bacchanal sans toga,
with a kicker of puffy eyes
and bloated cheeks at school drop-off,
No more, Dionysius, no more.

From the Depths

When pebbles glowed
from the stern caress of
the water's churn
that echoed like an argument,

And grackles lingered
with eyes slick as a storm trooper's,
keening from boredom,
nothing to quell the starkness
of their winter view,

She took her husk of a heart
out for a stroll,
let the frigid damp seep in,
toes tasting brine,
a chill zippering up through tibia,
femur and sacred column of bone,
flooding the emptiness with pink slush.

Then she remembered—
some creatures can survive
for a time
in both fresh and salt water,
like certain crocodiles,
strange rays with razor spikes,
and legions of the recently un-loved.

Here We Are

I always knew we'd end up here,
even as I held you for the first time,
my cream-cheese covered newborn
with copper hair, a lusty cry,
and cowboy-ready legs kicking
into a bright, fluorescent world.

I just didn't know it would come so fast,
your waving goodbye,
a knowing smile on your lips
that says you understand
that this is harder for me
than it is for you.

You stand at the precipice of your life,
I've shared it with you lo these many years,
but it was always yours, and yours alone,
even as I cheered at soccer games and guitar recitals,
cried with you over broken bones and mean girls,
lounged together through endless Harry Potter weekends.

It's a love affair not to be repeated in this lifetime—

I'm on the sidelines now,
where I belong, still cheering,
but the field is yours,
to do with as you will,
to make a life that can hold all

the wonders of who you are,
to cobble together work that makes you proud,
makes you money,
but most importantly,
makes your heart sing.

We mothers may nag and overprotect,
but we are fierce
when it comes to the happiness
of our ducklings.
We want it all for you,
to go into the world full of chutzpah
and common sense,
to make mistakes, take chances,
(within reason, please)
to reap the bounty of your dreams,
all the while knowing that
the cheering section never sleeps,
the door is always open,
and warm cookies will be made on demand.

Whispers

The Bone Yard

Take me to the place
where your dreams died,
where oily black birds caw
and snaggle-beaked uglies
sniff out their next meal.
They gather in knots
on the branches above,
expectant mourners
waiting for you to turn your back
on your dreams—
the ones that squawk with a hunger for tomorrow,
that lope out of pale shadows
too timid to make eye contact.
The watchers scratch and twitch
waiting for your nerve to fail,
your treasure to be abandoned, again—
your untended dreams left to bloat in the sun.
Their feasting rattles the bones
like a shaman foretelling the future,
dreams lie desiccated in heaps,
bleached, forgotten,
cackling a tale of what might have been.

Processing Imperfections over Lunch

I don't need a mirror to study
my imperfections,
count my flaws,
catalogue my failings.
My friends are here to do it for me

over grilled chicken and Caesar salad—
Not overtly, not with malice aforethought,
we're here to catch up, right?
I love them and they love me
but our tribe is steeped in self-loathing,
reflecting back infinitely upon each of us,
like a carnival funhouse.

The ritualistic flagellation,
warped perceptions
of bellies and wrinkles,
the *less-than* status updates,
light chatter,
self-deprecating banter.
We pass the whip,

I'm small and imperfect,
now your turn.
Bonding through bondage,
breaking ourselves down
to connect with the shards,
I'll take my salad with a glass of rosé,
its petal-soft pink
the color of blood and water.

Within

In a silver box
lined with softest velvet
deep within my ribs,
is a bird,
nestled, with eyes wide—
it flutters off
to do the things birds must do,
but returns, always,
the memory of us luring it back,
remembering what it is to love you.

F. Scott and Zelda in Retrograde

She whirled around him,
a sun indifferent to its worshippers,
upending the essential order,
a rogue star defying its orbit,
commanding light,
swallowing darkness,
the allure, magnetic.

He, a far-flung moon,
outwardly stable with a turbulent core,
no Sea of Tranquility for respite,
he split open boulders to release their secrets,
tatting whispers onto sheets of onion skin.

She, in search of gravity,
wrote, danced, painted,
gifts in glorious excess,
carving out an elliptical path all her own
in a vast, twinkling emptiness.

Together, their parallax too great,
near-collisions too frequent,
she pulled in chaos like a red giant.
He, ever remote as a lunar shadow—
their combustible reactions flared,
the night sky changed irrevocably,
a faint green light shining on.

The Dragon Days of Fall

October blazes in
like a trumpet fanfare,
fiery hues that light up the
landscape in bursts
of pumpkin, sunflower,
and berry red—
the greens of back-to-school sent packing.
Rogue days of Indian summer
will be overwhelmed by the insistent cool
as morning ushers in the chill,
reliable and welcome.
I step onto the porch and
let out a dramatic exhale
like a third grader at the bus stop,
my breath made visible,
a lone dragon
marveling at my fire.

On the Move

You know when it's time to go,
the walls tightening around you,
sharp edges gouging into
marshmallow body,
legs armored but exposed.
You curl up but
tender parts leak out,
open to the sea's bite.
Time to sidle up to a bigger shell,
bump into the hull, casually,
unobtrusively.
So sorry, you'll say
if a head pops out,
and keep scrabbling along,
leaving trails in the sand
like Foucault's pendulum,
searching for a place that fits—
a place to hold this
latest, bursting incarnation of you.

Force of Nature

She tore through gravity
like a machete through underbrush,
her plaid work shirt a blur of red and black,
pounding pillows
stacking plates—

I'd sit and build skyscrapers,
her footfalls, insistent toms toms above me
as water was turned on and off,
off and on.
She'd whirl back with a load of laundry,
plunk it next to my towers,

and for a few minutes she'd stop,
plaid holding steady,
a cross-legged tornado
folding towels and t-shirts.
I'd belly flop into the basket of warm clothes,
and she'd make the rarest of sounds—

A laugh that challenged even
the swishy clang of the dishwasher—
bounced off the kitchen cabinets
and landed in the soft tissue of memory,
just the two of us, together,
in a moment scooped
out of the drudge.

Ocean Weary

Salt air has a quality unlike
city air, mountain air, desert air.
Beyond the brininess,
it's the taste of abandon—
the thrill of past-your-bedtime shenanigans,
leaping off sea-walls in nightgowns
that balloon out like lazy jellyfish—
a splashdown of sand and giggles,
blowing bubbles sure to break records
if only you can outrun your brother's hand,
the dead-tiredness after a day at the beach,
sand still chafing between your toes
as you flop onto a stiff bunk bed
that feels like a pile of autumn leaves
raked just for you.

The Buoyancy of Secrets

They will rise,
like a bloated corpse,
a balloon held under water,
a splinter wriggling into sight.
Secrets have a gravity all their own,
as heavy as they are light—
the plutonium of memory,
contaminating from within.

Visiting Sparrows

Relativity

Gravity has a tighter grip
on some than others.
The angry, the critical
wear it like a lead vest
from the dentist's office.

Kids are the most unaffected,
like cosmonauts and hot air balloons,
their buoyancy feels ominous,
as if they could float off,
crash into baseball scoreboards,
get tangled in high tension wires,
or hook onto the Eiffel tower with a sticky grab.

They're tethered to earth only
by their parents' love
and a yearning to become something
as yet unknown
but hinted at in their dreams.

Morning Walk

I duck out of an October sun
that makes rooftops smolder
like a leaf about to catch fire.
The trail is damp and
all around me life is transitioning,
the collision of seasons peeling back,
making room,
stages of birth, death, grief,
and a thousand nuances in between.

Sounds muffled yet amplified,
the low hum of life interrupted
by sporadic riffs,
the shriek of a blue jay,
a crow flaunting its oily wings,
acorns popping underfoot.

Light filters through the canopy,
throwing random spotlights—
a toadstool,
a pile of brush,
a chipmunk caught center stage—
unwitting players in a production
that has no end.

Oaks stand tall along the path,
trunks splashed with circles of moss,
like a boy who couldn't outrun a snowball fight.
A fallen branch blocks my way,
its cinnamon leaves draped,

curved like the line of dancer's back.
I take an unfamiliar path

to find a swamp burning in the morning rays—
the mist above the fulminating cattails
a helpful Lazarus,
a landscape rises in slow motion,
the flotsam and jetsam of new life
drifting towards creation.

The Snob

Inside me lives a snob
in a velvet smoking jacket,
ready to snark, to condescend,
to outline my foibles in rich detail
between sips of sherry,
expound on my inadequacies
in an accent worthy of Masterpiece Theatre,

His lids at permanent half-mast,
he sighs at my frightful incompetence,
delights in my failings,
my extra ten pounds,
my fear of being exposed.

He offers me a seat in the
wing-back chair next to his,
to watch life from the sidelines,
join the cozy critic's corner,
the aroma of raisins
strong and sweet.

A Vanishing

Gravestones slick and grey,
sugar maples sigh
like teenagers in full mope,
rain nudges the leaves
to kiss the damp earth,
a teasing courtship dance
the cool air will consummate
soon enough,
rivulets snake down
carefully carved epitaphs,
skulls and angels,
snippets of prayer,
dates of arrival and departure,
erasing lives written in stone.
Preachers,
pioneers of industry,
ship captains,
mothers, sisters,
mourned only by the dead,
no dahlias or posies left behind.
A stray violet may grieve in spring,
as dandelions, ever-loyal,
gather around the off-kilter stones.

The Archer's Paradox

Body taut as a bowstring,
muscles straining towards calm
as focus contracts to a pinhole.
Aim locked on a dancing mote of air
hovering just above the circle's edge.
Then the moment nods—
pupils track the arrow
toward its clown-colored destination,
a Mondrian of circles radiating out.
Then the gasp of penetration,
the exhale of mindful effort—
As with anything much desired,
it's all in the release, the letting go.
Want it too much,
strain too hard,
and we overshoot,
yanking the arrow from its natural path—
past the target
to claim tree
or dandelion
or barn door with its point.

A Benediction

An eager supplicant strokes
the velvet rope, anxious,
muttering like a novice with her rosary,
foreign phrases that
divulge her darkest secrets

to those in black
who dole out the healing hosts,
dispensers of a balm protected
behind walls of glass and gold.
She steps forward,

eyes raised in a half-question,
a riot of pastels laid in perfect rows
before her,
desires tumble out—
chocolate, citron, framboise.
Nimble fingers slip

holy discs into boxes of pale green.
A nod dismisses her down the line
where she sleepwalks
through the tally,
tipsy from the perfumed air.

She steps
into the Paris street,
fumbling with the seal.

She lifts the host in silent prayer,
and lets it find her tongue.

A communion of chocolate
and acolyte,
bliss in one bite,
There is a god
and his name is Ladurée.

Quickening

What secrets live in the
downiest parts of your soul,
in the airy spaces where
conditions are just so?

A Goldilocks Zone
where doubt fizzles like wafting embers
and critics bite their tongue bloody,
where lungs fill with the salted air of ease,
where secrets, nestled in like perfect eggs,
hold the truth of who you are,
whole and precious and loved.

A force formidable and soft—
these secrets await
the moment of quickening,
the call to become,
the twitch that invites your destiny.

We Will Carry You Out

When the time comes,
we will carry you out,
with reverence and quiet dignity—
like Cleopatra through the streets of Alexandria,
like a bejeweled Maharini floating atop her entourage.

We will carry you out in a box lined with
the puckered satin of doll's clothes,
your lips stained fuchsia one last time,
as brass handles bite into our numb hands.

We will carry you out
to the banks of the River Styx,
across the fields of Elysium
where your soul can rest in the lavender
and your body can be whole again.

We will carry you out
heads bowed, eyes filled,
to send you on the next leg
of your journey
as bagpipes moan the wretched song
of your leaving.

St. Francis in the Garden

I love a saint with a bird on his head
carved from stone,
sanctifying the garden
so I'll sit awhile–
but don't expect me to crawl through glass
while you stand there watching

lilacs sway and slugs wander by.
You excelled at giving things up,
making amends with legendary grace,
but forgiveness is for saints
and loan sharks gone soft,
and I'm neither one, my chits all used up,

my Hail Mary's out of juice for debts
that can never be collected,
wrongs piled up like ketchup packets
and chopsticks in a junk drawer.
I hold on to past injustices
like a little girl and her threadbare rabbit,

the matted, smelly thing a comfort.
So let's enjoy the garden together,
you with your hardened perfection
and visiting sparrows,
and me with my bunny,
holding back the onslaught.

Acknowledgements

A version of these poems first appeared
in the following publications:

The Wild Word: "The Solace of Dirt," "Lost and Found," and "Tell Me"
Ink & Letters: "Vanishing Point"
The Phoenix Soul: "Cracks"
Wildness: Voices of the Sacred Landscape, Homebound Publications:
   "Up and Out" and "100 Inches and Counting"
Switchgrass Review: "Unspeakable"
The Binnacle, University of Maine: "Deflated" (Honorable
   Mention, Ultra-short Competition)
Brightly Press, Poetry Prize (3rd Place): "Dear Poetry Editor"
WSQ, Feminist Press: "On Demand" and "Processing
   Imperfections over Lunch"
Poeming Pigeon Anthology–Food Edition: "A Benediction"

I'd like to thank the loves of my life, Rick and Rory, whose bedrock
belief in me and my work helps get me to the page even when I feel
like a listless, no-talent sea sponge. Their clucks of encouragement
and surprise chocolate treats make all the difference.

I'm grateful for the friendship and support of Amy Baltzell, Maile
Black, Rod Kessler, Jody Davis, Kathryn and David Hayward, Dana
Hyland, Jeff Flaherty, Susan Haltmaier, Ann Cavanaugh, Nancy
Webster, my ever-texting Flaherty siblings (Sue, Dick, Kathleen,
and Joanne), Mitch Norcross, Rebecca Carman, Susan Smith, Kar-
en Kline, Leslie Seaton Malis, Sean Murphy, Ronnie Citron-Fink,
Kelley McGee-Souza, my Bread Loaf and Noepe compadres, and
the Andover Poet Laureate Council.

About the Author

Linda Flaherty Haltmaier is an award-winning writer and the Poet Laureate of Andover, Massachusetts. She is the winner of the Homebound Publications Poetry Prize for her full-length collection, *Rolling up the Sky* (2016). Her work has earned numerous awards including first place in the Palm Beach Poetry Festival Competition, finalist honors for both the Princemere Poetry Prize and the Tucson Festival of the Book Literary Award, and been shortlisted for the Robert Frost Poetry Prize. She has been nominated for a Pushcart Prize and her poems have appeared extensively in journals and anthologies including *Switchgrass Review, WSQ, Ink & Letters, Wild Word*, and more. Her debut chapbook, *Catch and Release*, was published by Finishing Line Press (2015). A Harvard graduate, Linda has received writing residencies at the Noepe Center for the Literary Arts and been a poetry contributor at the Bread Loaf Writers' Conference. As Poet Laureate, Linda leads poetry workshops, gives readings, and promotes poetry on the North Shore of Boston where she lives with her husband and daughter.

HOMEBOUND PUBLICATIONS

Ensuring that the mainstream isn't the only stream.

At Homebound Publications, we publish books written by independent voices for independent minds. Our books focus on a return to simplicity and balance, connection to the earth and each other, and the search for meaning and authenticity. Founded in 2011, Homebound Publications is one of the rising independent publishers in the country. Collectively through our imprints, we publish between fifteen to twenty offerings each year. Our authors have received dozens of awards, including: *Foreword Reviews'* Book of the Year, Nautilus Book Award, Benjamin Franklin Book Awards, and Saltire Literary Awards. Highly-respected among bookstores, readers and authors alike, Homebound Publications has a proven devotion to quality, originality and integrity.

We are a small press with big ideas. As an independent publisher we strive to ensure that the mainstream is not the only stream. It is our intention at Homebound Publications to preserve contemplative storytelling. We publish full-length introspective works of creative non-fiction as well as essay collections, travel writing, poetry, and novels. In all our titles, our intention is to introduce new perspectives that will directly aid humankind in the trials we face at present as a global village.

WWW.HOMEBOUNDPUBLICATIONS.COM

CPSIA information can be obtained
at www.ICGtesting.com
Printed in the USA
LVHW03s0537080918
589426LV00001B/69/P